anythink

Pebble® Plus

· HOLIDAY HISTORIES ·

A Short History of
THANKSGIVING

by *Sally Lee*

Consulting Editor: Gail Saunders-Smith, PhD

Consultant: Jeannine Diddle Uzzi, PhD,
Director of Faculty Programs,
Associated Colleges of the South

CAPSTONE PRESS
a capstone imprint

Pebble Plus is published by Capstone Press,
1710 Roe Crest Drive, North Mankato, Minnesota 56003
www.capstonepub.com

Library of Congress Cataloging-in-Publication Data
Lee, Sally.
  A short history of thanksgiving / by Sally Lee.
     pages cm.—(Pebble plus. Holiday histories)
  Includes bibliographical references and index.
  ISBN 978-1-4914-6097-9 (library binding)—ISBN 978-1-4914-6101-3 (pbk.)—
ISBN 978-1-4914-6105-1 (ebook pdf)
1. Thanksgiving Day—Juvenile literature. I. Title.
  GT4975.L4 2016
  394.2649—dc23   2015002030

Editorial Credits
Erika L. Shores, editor; Bobbie Nuytten, designer; Kelly Garvin, media researcher;
Lori Barbeau, production specialist

Photo Credits
Alamy: MBI, 5, Jim West, 21; Corbis/Stapleton Collection, 15; Mary Evans Picture Library, 19;
North Wind Picture Archives, 9, 11, Nativestock, 7; Science Source/Photo Researchers, 13;
Shutterstock: demarcomedia, cover, Everett Historical, 19 (inset), onot, cover (leaves),
The First Thanksgiving/1621 Oil Painting by Karen Rinaldo, 17

Design Elements: Shutterstock/redstone

Note to Parents and Teachers

The Holiday Histories set supports national curriculum standards for social studies. This book describes
and illustrates the holiday of Thanksgiving. The images support early readers in understanding the text.
The repetition of words and phrases helps early readers learn new words. This book also introduces early
readers to subject-specific vocabulary words, which are defined in the Glossary section. Early readers may
need assistance to read some words and to use the Table of Contents, Glossary, Read More, Internet Sites,
Critical Thinking Using the Common Core, and Index sections of the book.

Printed in the United States of America in North Mankato, Minnesota.
042015   008823CGF15

Table of Contents

Giving Thanks

Thanksgiving is a day to show thanks for what we have. Every family has ways to honor the day. These traditions come from events that happened long ago.

People have held fall festivals
for thousands of years. Farmers
gathered their crops. Then they
had a big meal. It showed
their thankfulness for the harvest.

Coming to America

Today's Thanksgiving began
with a group of people
from England. They wanted
to start a new church apart
from the Church of England.

In 1620 the English group set sail on the *Mayflower*. The 102 people on board were crowded, hungry, and sick.

The *Mayflower* arrived at today's state of Massachusetts. The first winter was cold and terrible. There was little food. Nearly half of the English settlers died.

Growing Food

In spring native people helped
the English settlers. The Wampanoag
taught them to plant corn, beans,
and squash. The Wampanoag
also helped the settlers hunt.

In 1621 the settlers wanted
to show thanks for the fall harvest.
Ninety native people joined them.
They ate, danced, and played
games for three days.

A U.S. Holiday

In 1863 President Abraham Lincoln made Thanksgiving an official U.S. holiday. Now it's always held the fourth Thursday in November.

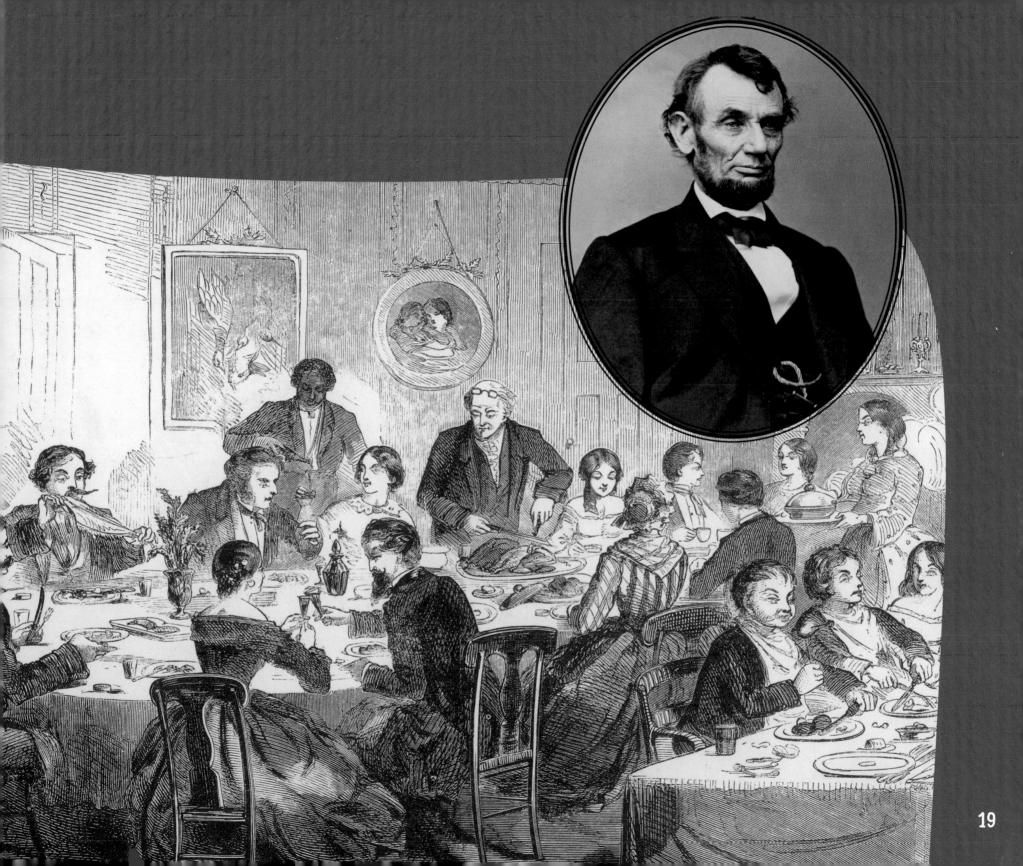

Thanksgiving still means family, food, and games. People watch football on TV. Others serve food to the needy. Most of all the holiday reminds us to be grateful.

Glossary

crop—a plant farmers grow in large amounts, usually for food

grateful—thankful

harvest—the gathering of a crop

holiday—a day on which work, school, or any regular activities are officially stopped

native—belonging to a place

official—to be approved by someone who holds a position in government

settler—a person who makes a home in a new place

tradition—a custom handed down from parents to children over many years

Read More

Herrington, Lisa M. *Thanksgiving.* Rookie Read-About Holidays. New York: Children's Press, 2013.

McGee, Randel. *Paper Crafts for Thanksgiving.* Paper Craft Fun for Holidays. Berkeley Heights, N.J.: Enslow, 2013.

Rissman, Rebecca. *Thanksgiving.* Holidays and Festivals. North Mankato, Minn.: Heinemann-Raintree Library, 2011.

Internet Sites

FactHound offers a safe, fun way to find Internet sites related to this book. All of the sites on FactHound have been researched by our staff.

Here's all you do:

Visit *www.facthound.com*

Type in this code: 9781491460979

Check out projects, games and lots more at
www.capstonekids.com

Critical Thinking
Using the Common Core

1. What were the people at the first Thanksgiving thankful for? What are you and your family thankful for today? (Key Ideas and Details)

2. What might have happened to the English settlers if the Wampanoag hadn't helped them? (Integration of Knowledge and Ideas)

Index

Word Count: 222
Grade: 1
Early-Intervention Level: 18